POETRY FOR HUMANITY.
CHRONICLES OF LIFE
IN LOCKDOWN

ExLibric

JUAN ANTONIO ALMANADO

POETRY FOR HUMANITY.
CHRONICLES OF LIFE
IN LOCKDOWN

EXLIBRIC

ANTEQUERA 2020

JUAN ANTONIO ALMANADO

POETRY FOR HUMANITY.
CHRONICLES OF LIFE
IN LOCKDOWN

Acknowledgements

I cannot and must not forget to thank all the people who have helped with their advice and encouragement to achieve the completion of this work, in an important stage of my life, as it is my first publication. Special thanks to my sister-in-law Nazareth and my friend Pilar, a literature professor, both for their wise advice; to my son Adrian, who has always supported me and read my work; to my daughter-in-law Noelia, who designed the front and back covers; to my family and to all those friends who, through their reading, have encouraged me to bring this collection of poems to fruition. Without them I would have lacked the courage to complete this book.

Translated into English with love and dedication
by María Duquenne.

Foreword

One day, early in the morning. One of those days when I still could see your pretty smile on your beautiful face and not only your sincere eyes, but the morning of that day, got a bad twist, then also the afternoon and night, the night was growing longer, never ending, and more and more distant, making us forget the feeling our daily routine.

The news became monotonous and sad, so sad that it did not seem of this world, although we would have liked to wake up from that senseless nightmare. And since that dark day, our existence has been changed for worse or who knows for better, if it weren't for all those who were defeated and who had been deprived of hope, and even worse for the loved ones who saw their lives skewed.

Later, with empty hands and a heart and mind full of that lost hope, souls went in search of the radiance to be able to win the last battle, and so the days went by accumulating wars won but also yet lost.

Little by little, we left behind our dreary lies along the way, and in this way they helped to clear the shadows of the path, to enter into the true essence of life, also of the importance of valuing things for their true merit and not for the superfluous value of all that in the past we had hoarded as treasure in our lives.

This book of poems tries to transmit the feelings of its author and is written, not only for lovers of poetry, but also for the rest of humanity, as it addresses each of the sectors and feelings involved in the covid19 and in a predominant way, to honour, also to criticize all those who, in one way or another, helped forge the memory of our chronicle for the pages of the history books of a near and yet distant future in which our ancestors should reflect on in order to put an end to this pandemic of men blinded by power and abandoned by humanity.

On the other hand, the author includes in this book two short stories, in different volumes, referring in the first one to the monotony of confinement and in the second one to the difficulties of a love relationship, with a slight sense of eroticism between a couple, of an almost withered marriage, real as life itself, linking subtly both stories.

Letter of a nightmare

The sun slipped through unannounced, between the slats of the half-open shutters. Perhaps in the past, I would have put my hand over my face to shield it from the rays of light, but for days, I had been accustomed not to let it touch me. It was a matter of trying to stay safe and sound from that virus which was totally rocking the pillars of humanity.

I got out of bed, got dressed, and wore my lucky pyjamas, the ones I was wearing early one morning, when I received the happy news of my imminent start to my new job. I needed to hold on to something in order to survive that distressing situation, although the concern of not catching the disease was stronger for the people I had to protect, than for myself. Alvaro lived alone. He had recently broken off his relationship with his partner, after ten long years, full of sincere love, although destitute of routine. But things are as they are and if the flame goes out, it is necessary to move on to let the ashes fly.

As I took my last sip of coffee, I turned on the television, to hear, for sure, the incessant bombardment of news about the so-called «bug» that had the world in fear, leading it to a humanitarian and economic crisis that is still incalculable today, two months after the accursed disease had befallen so many people. Each day that passed became more uncertain, the light could hardly be seen at the end of the tunnel.

Out of the corner of my eye, with great amazement, I took a look at that speaker who naturally told the news. He was talking about the independence of Catalonia, about a new case of gender-based violence, about some criminals who had robbed a bank on the outskirts of Madrid. People were swarming the streets freely and the reporter was not wearing a mask, he was not covering his microphone with plastic either and not a single reference to the coronavirus, I changed the channel a bit angrily, a lack of sensitivity was not possible. In these difficult moments the most important thing was to keep us informed about the pandemic that was afflicting everyone. My eyes were as open as they were surprised by what I was hearing in the sports section.

—In the match played yesterday in Italy after the expulsion of Sergio Ramos, Real Madrid won 3 to 0 to the dreaded Inter - at the end of the game the crowd gathered at the gates of the stadium to scold the referee after pointing out a controversial penalty.

This time I could not help rubbing my eyes with my hands, full of disbelief. On the way to the shower, I thought about whether I was going mad, after a few minutes brooding under the running water, I rushed to get dressed, that police uniform was weighing more and more heavily on my conscience, the responsibility I knew was expected of me in that outfit sometimes overtook me. I went down the stairs almost without stepping on the steps and without touching the handrail, it had been days since I had not taken the elevator for safety.

The radio station was turned on automatically when I started the car. During the discussion, they talked about Minister Abalos and the lack of responsibility for having met with Maduro's "number two". Although it seemed like a totally logical story, I was once again overwhelmed, my disgruntled mind could not understand what was going on.

The mobile phone rang before I left the parking and a chill ran through my skin. I couldn't believe it, my great friend Isaac was calling me, it wasn't possible, yesterday I left him in the hospital struggling between life and death plugged into a respirator and the doctors no longer treated him.

The Ruiz family greeted me as they passed in front of me, as if the alert wasn't their problem.

Alvaro went out slowly in fear, expecting to see the loneliness of the sidewalks and longing for the smell of pollution on the streets of Madrid. Car traffic had slowed down so much that you could hear the noisy song of some little bird caused by the newly arrived spring.

In a park near the parking, several children played ball, while the mothers chatted in a relaxed attitude about their chores, sitting on the surrounding benches. The terraces of the adjoining bars were full of customers and reflected the hustle and bustle of the city. He didn't understand anything, what was going on? Just yesterday when he was returning home after a busy day, there was the most austere peace he had ever seen in his neighbourhood.

Suddenly, he heard a deafening thudding sound on the four white walls of his room. The alarm clock that ferociously sounded from his bedside table, caused a burst in his heart that made him wake up agitated from the wonderful dream he was enjoying.

The sun slipped through unannounced, between the slats of the half-open shutters. Perhaps in the past, he would have put his hand over his face to shield it from the rays of light, but for days, he had been accustomed not to let it touch him. It was a matter of trying to stay safe and sound from that virus which was totally rocking the pillars of humanity.

The laziness and tiredness of the last few days encouraged him to stay in the comfortable bed a little longer, but his responsibility made him get up in a hurry.

As he took his last sip of coffee, he turned on the television, to hear, for sure, the incessant bombardment of news about the so-called «bug» that had the world in fear, leading it to a humanitarian and economic crisis that is still incalculable today, two months after the accursed disease had befallen so many people. Each day that passed became more uncertain, but yet the end of the tunnel seemed closer and the light could almost be seen.

He made an effort to listen to what common sense wanted to tell him, but that speaker who quietly told the news, spoke of the coronavirus... that the contagions had decreased and that the apex of the pyramid had been reached and that the number of cured people was growing more and more all over the world. He also thanked the citizens for remaining most of the time in their homes and that leaders of all countries had united to defeat the dreaded virus together. A reporter was interviewing the head of the medical service with his microphone covered in thin plastic, just as a large number of discharged patients were walking out the door of the hospital. He changed the channel a bit angrily, despite the optimism of the day's news, it was not the news he wanted to hear. There was no football, no talk of politics, not even of the odd robbery, which he would have liked to have heard under those circumstances.

On the way to the shower, he kept thinking about how to escape from that nightmare that haunted him night after night, madness lurking somewhere in his mind.

In the parking he didn't exchange any greetings and his great friend Isaac didn't call him.

The streets and parks remained empty before Alvaro's impassive gaze, he didn't want to believe that this was happening again. The terraces devoid of tables and chairs, cried because of the absence of customers, and the silence of the sidewalks melted with the deserted asphalt of noisy vehicles that didn't leave their pleasant smell of burning fuel among the wind and the bustle of their people. For a moment, he realized the tremendous non-sense that had just passed through his mind: the pleasant smell of burning fuel? He! A staunch defender of nature who had so often ranting about keeping the air clean and pure wanting to pollute the air that was being breathed lately!

The day was long and tedious, but he was finally returning home so that he could rest again. He longed to fall asleep, it was the only way to break through the unbearable chaos he was exposed to every day. He climbed the stairs almost without stepping on the steps and without touching the handrail, the elevator had disappeared from his daily routine.

The sun slipped through unannounced, between the slats of the half-open shutters. Perhaps in the past, I would have put my hand over my face to shield it from the rays of light, but for days, I had been accustomed not to let it touch me. It was a matter of trying to stay safe and sound from that virus which was totally rocking the pillars of humanity.

Life was going on and Alvaro was not going to let go of it, without finishing his mission in that crisis he had to deal with, just like the rest of the citizens, in spite of the work he had been entrusted with in Carabanchel, one of the most dangerous districts of Madrid.

As he took his last sip of coffee, he couldn't help but remember the words of his great friend and co-worker Isaac, a lover of history, shortly before he fell ill, from being infected during a fight with a criminal who had symptoms of coronavirus.

—I can't believe that in 1943 the Americans were able to create a tank every 5 minutes, in the middle of the 20th century, with infinitely less technology than we have today and now, at the dawn of the 21st century, we are not able to manufacture thousands, I mean not thousands, but millions of masks to protect all the people on earth and create enough respirators so that nobody dies for lack of them, just like the tests and the Individual Protection Equipments. —He looked very angry, meanwhile he put his elbow before coughing a second time.

Alvaro shook his head from side to side several times, wanting to get rid of Isaac's wise words and escape from his memories, which reverberated like a hammer in his mind. He preferred to spend his energies thinking about how to help his friend's widow, who had left two young children orphaned.

Today, it was almost four months since the accursed disease had unquestionably overtaken the social welfare.

The background sound of the television was heard in the kitchen-dining room of the small apartment, the speaker narrated the news of the day with more euphoria than usual: the number of infections had dropped considerably, as had the number of people in the ICU and the number of victims, but Álvaro, like the rest of the world, wondered how the world population would return to normal and tried to be optimistic. He was in favour of the fact that the struggle should not be aimed at an immediate return to the usual routine because the usual routine had proved ineffective in society, but should focus on learning from the mistakes made and fighting against the virus in order to return with all our strength and change the usual routine for something more humane and safer.

Suddenly a glimmer of light came to his mind, he had been thinking for several days about an article he had read from some well-known scientist about the discomfort of the virus at temperatures over 26° and with 85% humidity, with those conditions the virus succumbed. So! Why not create a cabin similar to the one with sun rays, with a hot air blower and a dehumidifier and which also has a thermal camera to detect body temperature, which could be installed at the entrance of each of the establishments that have a considerable attendance and in which, before entering that place, people would enter for an instant? I could call it «covi-des».

Alvaro was a very imaginative person who liked to fantasize sometimes with his implausible ideas and other times not so much, he always tried to look for the bright side of things, so in his internal battle that he fought every day between good and evil, he gave a breath of hope to humanity. He was the typical person who thought that the coronavirus would not only counteract lives, but also save them, the sudden fall of contamination would contribute to this, freeing many children and elderly people from a fateful outcome in the future.

On the other hand, he was thinking about the fragility of human beings: «We are just a grain of sand in the great mountain of life, this virus has left the supposed robustness of man on earth up in the air. We thought we were the navel of the world and nothing could be further from the truth, overnight we stopped showing off and broke into a thousand pieces like a porcelain figure when it crashed to the ground».

The unmistakable melody of the pop song «I will survive» woke him up from his rapture with a jump, it came from the speakers of his mobile phone, on the other side of the phone he could hear the broken voice of his partner Ramon.

—Alvaro, from tomorrow the state of confinement will be history, the population will be able to start leaving their homes, although taking extreme precautions. —Alvaro's overflowing joy gave way to eyes full of tears of emotion.

The sun slipped through unannounced, between the slats of the half-open shutters. Perhaps in the past, I would have put my hand over my face to shield it from the rays of light, but it had been days since I had allowed myself to feel the sun again. The virus proved not to be as evil as people imagined.

The television spoke of how, despite the more than 28,000 victims and the great mourning it had caused in the families of those people, the percentage of the population with a fatal end had not been as tremendous as expected. This percentage was even more valuable for people from the age of 80 onwards, so the authorities decided to continue confining these people at risk and releasing the rest of the population, but with some restrictions and security measures.

Alvaro's face oozed with happiness and hope. May humanity have learned the great lesson that life has given us. Meanwhile, a phrase that he always liked to utter in the worst moments, just like its author the great poet Antonio Machado, was tinkling in his mind: «Today is always still».

Although, on the other hand, I couldn't stop thinking about the loneliness he was immersed in, after his failed marriage...

POETRY FOR HUMANITY
CHRONICLES OF LIFE
IN LOCKDOWN

I. TO THOSE WHO LEFT US

The wind has blown you away,
dragging happiness
like a leaf that flies aimlessly
in the path of darkness.
So now what?,
if I don't know how to live without you.
Now I have lost everything too
because I was covered by you.
You left me with nothing but melancholy
and a broken heart
wilfully wandering here and there,
unwillingly to anchor it with care
not to cry anymore,
trying to put my soul back together
with little bits of tenacity,
muted by this cruelty.

A glance here and there.
The light that always shone is gone;
gone with the morning to walk its sadness
through the corridors of your memories.
I close my eyes and try to imagine you
here, again at my side.
You're there, I can't touch you,
but I can feel you inside.
I can't see you, but I can smell you.

And what else would I want... to have you.
You left me empty-handed,
searching in the attic of my mind
a convincing explanation
although I may... never find it.

Amidst the silence of some nightmares
and the sound of a bitter crying,
only broken by helplessness
of this pain that gnaws at my conscience
for not being able to hold a vigil after your absence,
the house becomes smaller
feeling that you won't come back.
I need to seek peace
from heaven… even beyond.
Perhaps time will heal the fatigue of so much grief.

II. TO HEALTH WORKERS

Heart of fire, self-sacrificing feeling,
tell me where are you, as I haven't found you.
Faded into oblivion in the past
and idolised overnight.

Who saw you and who sees you.
Yesterday, leaf in the haystack
and ashes at the stake,
today, jewel in the trousseau
and flame in the brazier.

The afternoon dies until the dawn,
between a corridor and a soft rest.
Fatigue sleeps in haven of peace
while the night is looking for calm.

What you were, you will not be,
one day the people will speak,
the sooner you come
of your random exploits.

III. TO THE CARRIERS

Loneliness is my companion corroded
over the path of the road,
through the mountain,
water had long gone dry in the fountain.

Sometimes I cry in your absence
the moments we did not live,
watching over your presence
and my poor heart filled
with your love in abstinence.

Don't cry for my essence,
my poor morning heart.
You know of your impatience
as the day departs.

People wave as I arrive
with a grateful smile.
May God grant me strength
at my final breath.

Happiness is the word
that gives light to my path.
With sleep I always can
dream that you can rest assured.

IV. TO THE OTHER HEROES

This poem is dedicated to the supermarkets' workers, shopkeepers, bakers, pharmacists and in general to all those who were there, despite their fears so that in our homes we lacked nothing.

I walk through the city
empty of its humankind,
in the fear of my mind
putting anxiety aside.

I clench my teeth and grin
whilst I struggle to maintain my serenity,
although the difficulty
helps me hold on tighter.

But now it's too late,
I wasn't born that way.
I didn't intend it either today,
nothing makes me flinch when I await.

The day goes by and in my head
there's only place
for the rather reluctant scare,
of my people,who are waiting
with bated breath.

Then... I go back to my fears,
in the shadows of the empty streets,
thinking about you and your stunts
and tricks
to get the virus off your tears.

I want you to remember me
as the hero I have never played,
but never forget... I never ran away,
even if the bug scares me.

V. TO THE SECURITY FORCES

A siren sounds
that breaks the silence
of the deserted streets
in these uncertain times.

You know me well enough
because I live among you
watching over you
during your times of misery.

You know that I play hide-and-seek,
to eliminate danger,
watching over you
hiding my fear or anger.

Your basic freedom
is born from my determination
to keep fighting,
often not knowing how,
not knowing when.

However, if a storm rages
honour, loyalty and overriding decency
can conquer evil.
And so if the risk demands
I would fight whoever

with the patience of a saint
as if it were a child's game.

I care for your safety
and at times valued,
but I am trying to improve
and always willing to help.

VI. TO THOSE LIKE LUIS

This poem is dedicated to a very dear person Luis Porras Sánchez, born in Montemayor (Córdoba). I did not have the opportunity to meet him in person, but I had the privilege of listening to his experiences in the words of his daughter Pilar, so that I esteem and love him.

The poem is taken from fragments written by him, which I have selected and marked between quotes, to complete them with my words of the deepest feelings about him, and I believe of his way of thinking, from what I have read of his books of haiku, short poems of Japanese origin, written from the depths of the soul.

Without a doubt, he was a good and wise man of the old school, of those who, with their effort and sweat, changed our beloved Spain, to give us a better life.

That life that we have denied during this pandemic to our elders, for the simple fact of belonging to a generation of the past, and now for sure, our life will never be the same as before.

There will never be another generation like this.

Time, what is time?
Without life, time means nothing.
When we are not here,
when the halo of the soul
leaves our body,
what are wails for?
«Yesterday is already gone,

today has not passed by
and tomorrow… tomorrow what?»
Tomorrow there will only be darkness,
we will be dust on the horizon
So… «don't cry over nothing,
save the tears that will be needed»,
so that your thoughts
resurface like a bird that takes flight
after its wings were clipped.
Be glad you are still alive
and look in the present
what will be absent
in the recent future.
«It is better to play deaf
if the news is so bitter»
because…
«we will all be wise in the final judgment».
Never doubt it, «don't cry over nothing,
save the tears as you will need them»,
and «if you are poor
don't worry so much, the clock is ticking».
Remember,
«the sobs and the diapers were trapped in the past».
Who does not respect those experiences
from yesterday and the past?
«Never worry so much,
time is running out»
and does not wait for any spring.

Luis Porras y J.A. Almanado

VII. TO THE MOTHER IN LOCKDOWN

If I mourn your absence,
is because I still sleep with your name
on my pillow,
seeking your presence,
that no longer exists in tales of wonder.

You never leave me in the dark alone
and when it is rainy,
you cover the sleepless nights with a mantle of hope,
filling the storm with tranquillity.

You could embrace heaven with your kindness,
but above your outspread wings with sweetness
you have all those hearts
for which you live with passion,
fighting with determination.

No one like you makes my feelings fly so high.
I want to imagine you close by,
to smell your mother's perfume
that will always remain in my memories in bloom.

Your hands tired of fighting for freedom
leave a mark when you pass by,

but you put aside your fantasies
to share the greatest thing about yourself
with those who one day
from your bowels
you gave birth to.

I want your shadow always in the orchard
where my dreams run into the light,
that light you give off when you walk,
that light you hide in your innermost.

No one like you makes my feelings fly so high.
I want to imagine you close by,

to smell your mother's perfume
that will always remain in my memories in bloom.

No one would say that you were one day
sunshine in my window,
today also moon
in my desolate nights.

I like to see your face when you smile,
wasting happiness
after having given your all
without asking for anything.

Your heart is so big
that it does not fit in the universe

I'm always looking for you and there you are
with your soul full of humanity.

I love you, Mom.

VIII. FREEDOM

Wind, cannot you see me?
Why I no longer fell the whisper of your breath?
I dream that I am awake away from death
playing through your ups and downs again, free.

The house is getting smaller
without feeling you in my face
when we walked together
without time challenging us in a race.

Nostalgia for the shadows of the trees
rocked with your breath
flies into loneliness
from this life in death.

The children don't play around anymore,
you don't blow on my back anymore,
you don't pull my hair anymore
rampaging the leaves on the ground.

Gardens cry out in desolation
with the gentle rocking of your caresses
and the roar of the waves lashing
the shores of the beaches
empty of people,
as we turned together
from the most enormous walk.

Now the distance keeps us apart
through no fault of yours,
although the clock is ticking fast
towards meeting the breeze at last.

IX. VIRUS

Mom, Mom! Do monsters exist?
No, son. They only exist in stories.
Then why are we afraid of him?
Because he's more dangerous
than the monster in your stories.

If you are not careful
he goes inside
and can end your life.

No one knows how he came,
nor his origin,
but everyone knows him
and he proceeds without leniency.

You can find him on the corner
and also in the kitchen.
Old, young and children,
everyone can fall.
Wash your hands
if you want to beat him.

X. KIDS

I spy with my little eyes.
Somewhere in the house,
whose name I do not care to remember,
they play and play and play together.

Fuss, dear fuss.
Do not abandon me, patience,
on the edge of absence
if I run out of words.

When they sleep
watch the silence in the corners
and also on the balconies and borders,
and the parents in the shadow try to avoid it.

Tomorrow morning
a new day will shine,
but soon it was getting dark
and they were still playing hard.

And so was the adventure
not to go mad
Do not believe in the Boogeyman,
but in your sanity.

XI. TO THE SELFEMPLOYED WORKERS

Sun in the sky in spring,
now eternally forgotten,
wooden soldiers and vile thing,
now firmly downtrodden.

Under the yoke of the State
we ride in fear,
waiting with our mates
the expected reinforcements to appear.

And so pass the hours,
one by one, no warriors, no flowers,
while they ignore us,
in our cold trench eager to have a shelter.

Ours movements scrutinised
from the battlefield,
always concerned
no frontline crossing without a shield.

Weak in isolation,
but strong in the army,
that's why the generals
cannot win the war
without organisation.

And so pass the hours,
one by one, no warriors, no flowers,
while they ignore us,
in our cold trench eager to have a shelter.

XII. HYMN TO FRIENDSHIP

Times becomes eternal
to come back to life.
Crazy winter goes infernal,
secluded after the strife.

How many times have we laughed
between courses?
How many times have we pacted
between noises?

I want to have you close
to hold you when you are hushed,
your sweat little face, even if you can't hear my voices
I want to have you close
to comfort you in your choices.

I need to see you,
tell you things face-to-face
strengthen myself and my embrace
with your kind of strange friendship lace.

People wouldn't say
that you are almost my sister,
although no one would doubt it
from that early age.
Tired of looking at you behind the window,

cold reflection of your fase,
words with no grace
and the perpetual metal shield used as a pillow.

I want to have you close
to hold you when you are hushed
your sweat little face, even if you can't hear my voices
I want to have you close
to comfort you in your choices.

XIII. TO OUR ELDERS

Words of wisdom from your heart
boil and fall apart.
You never left us in the way
but they forget your fate today.

Yesterday's memories
you taught telling your stories.
The world is now more cultured,
but less balanced.

There's no soul,
nor control,
our hands have no wisdom
and waste feelings without a goal,
more like droll humor.

Mornings will be eternal
without your morning walks
on the streets, with the grandchildren,
masking patience,
every day more discreet your presence.

You were never to blame
of the abandonment of that
so one uncertain day
now you are denied…
for your old age with shame.

XIV. FEARFUL SEX

I saw you yesterday.
Like an illusion
the wind was rocking your body,
and you were flying
invoking the lost thirst.
I caressed your breasts
eager for passion.
Although… you pulled away.
My fingers were slipping
brushing your lips
that didn't say anything…
because you pulled away.

Blessed illusion of mine!
I used to give my life for you
just a few days ago,
and now no one of us would give
a shred of feeling
because of our broken relationship,
since that damn meeting
with the fear of dealing
face to face with terror,
looking for us in the proximity,
to declare war… on our love,
because you pulled away.

Alone with my loneliness,
I count the hours
from the last minute
that you denied me mercilessly.
I miss those moments
of pleasure experienced in our nest
before that evening,
when life became so cruel
like waking up in the morning without your skin,
because you pulled away.

There are no longer long days
with your hair on the pillow.
There are only bitter moments
wrapped up in your bizarre jealousy,
but you said nothing,
but you pulled away.
So…
my lost fingers on your back
burned the fire of the soul
while the world stood still…
and you didn't pull away.

XV. TO THE POLITICAL CLASS

Dear hypocritical majesties,
dear deaf leaders,
a new day now is born for believers.
Today is the day of prayers and dignity
for your vassals' sanity.

Dearly beloved madmen of the desired power,
we have come this far
with pockets full of solidarity,
through the twisted road,
disoriented by the stars that guided us,
leaving a trail of uncertain paths
and the empty saddlebags for all that talk,
even though no one knew it.

I see dignitaries who rule
blinded by consistency
We will have to beg for coherency
and demand the forgotten promises,
never accomplished
since that faraway day
that we put our trust in your hands and way.

Dear General Courts,
today I ask you to bring to my tree
the wisdom I need

to get life back on track
and so my dreams,
will not be shattered dreams
for your jaded foolishness.
And to be able to reach the future
full of hope,
surrounded by children and grandchildren,
even if you lack matureness.

Is useless at the moment
facing your opponent
among the ideals
and your purposes,
tired of your brazen arrogance
if you whip the proletarian.

Whilst I continue to be a prisoner
so that you and your silliness
fight heartless,
neglecting the real reason…
The welfare of the compromiser.

XVI. TO POVERTY

Because life became like that,
I've been looking for a shelter
in the shadow of the riddle
I have had to live for ever.

Now my world doesn't exist as it was.
Time is running slow
in this huge hall
of poor people waiting by my side.

I look at the past with longing,
because today's belongings
are a chimera.
And if I look into the future regretfully,
maybe I would see it differently.

So, when it gets dark like this,
my disconsolate thoughts,
are short of breath
at the tortuous recess
scared by uncertain fate.

I never imagined walking
by this unjust darkness,
distressed by the calamity
of my sad discomfort.

XVII

Undoubtedly there has been a lot of brave people during this pandemic, here we can make a gesture to thank the cooks and people who are offering their services in solidarity to feed all those in need.

There is no round table,
nor a squire to a knight,
in that place where I wait for you in the daylight
with the deepest hope, stout strong and able.

Wherever you are,
come and see me
I will take care of you so far,
I will make sure you don´t get sick or mad.

There is no greater satisfaction
than your consolation,
if I manage to refuse the duel.
I pray to God not to be cruel.

I feel like I am in heaven,
comforted by hope.
I don't want to be forgiven
for staying awake.

Money… Money is useless.
I just miss expressions of friendliness

and that you come as a breath of fresh air,
without the smell of a stranger somewhere.

Your empty hands
fill me with misery
for that great despondency
when you were hiding…
unexplainedly.

Never doubt yourself,
of what you once were.
You will soon stop being sad, for sure,
because you'll get out of this one, too.

XVIII. SOLITUDE

How many times have I hated you
in the darkness of my living room,
talking to myself from my gloom
pretty discouraged by my doom.

Between the cruel dawn
of a new day,
distorted by joy
as the evening goes away.

Faithful reflection of yesterday
with the same monotony,
also from the irony,
because it is scary when it gets dark.

What do you want me to tell you
if there is nothing new to tell?
Just a long thud
and the humming of the mind in the mud.

When I sleep owning
my most uncertain terrors
on the trail of reverie
to cure my ills and memories.

I look myself in the mirror.
I am the same as always,
though a little older
and a bit less eloquent nowadays.

Now my revenge has come.
I will never return in your treacherous trace,
because time taught me... to lie to you
to reach the fruit of hope.

XIX. LOVE IN THE DISTANCE

Today I realized
that my life without you
it is not happy anymore,
because without you, my love,
life has a different colour.
The sky is filled with black clouds
when you are not by my side
and I suffer from pure torment.

Today I realized
that you are my life, love.
For so long
I had you forgotten and abandoned desperately.
And in your loneliness you suffered disconsolately
without anyone looking after you.
The course of ambition
blinded me, barely any distraction,
playing through lies
with the person you admire.

Today I realized
that your world turned sad
and yet you never argued or went mad.
Now I look at your face
like a stranger,
looking for what you have changed

locked in your mind and protected.
From your loneliness
you call for calm,
so close to your soul
for too much coldness.

Today I realized, my love,
that my loneliness is comparable to yours,
and may life destroy me
like a burning sun
if I don't have your warmth.

I don't know if today will be to late
and if in your universe
there is still room for both of us,
in the return for hope
of a new alliance
between your life and my heart.

XX. FEAR

I don't want to see you.
when you come near.
Get away, I am stronger
than you fear.

If you suspect that I am finished,
don't stop, run away from me,
forget about what I was,
because from you I am free.

Face to fase, with dignity,
I will face you again.
You no longer frighten my will,
no matter how hard you try to give me pain.

I think of you in the distance.
Just with my thoughts you bow down to me.
Don't have any attachments to my existence
nor to my soul for its arrogance.

Yesterday you were a bad dream,
I used to hide under my screen,
feeling you on my back,
without attacks.

Today I fiercely dare you
and I laugh hard at you

as the only thing you have been doing so far
is to make me braver
so you will end up being devoured by a stranger.

XXI. TO VOLUNTEERS

One ant told the other.
«Let's join forces
to help the world together
with our hardest effort ever».

«But… it is a runaway crossroads.
You will have to fight the giant
by confronting an aberrant Monster.
You'd better… sit tight and be stronger.

The rain will come, so the fury.
You will not see it on the glass truly
and it will try to drag you down with its flow
down the path of misery».

«But difficulty is meaningless
to impose humanness
if the fatigue could be carried away,
at least, in my own way.

I am capable of moving mountains
in order to raise a smile,
with honour and pride,
to accomplish this huge task.

If I can't win instantly,
isolated, from this side,

I will fight with the help of the infantry
united by the force of pride».

On the podium there is no greater prestige
if the work is achieved
of one more round of applause,
by those you will save.

And even though we don't win the monster,
with our efforts… we will conquer.

XXII. HUGS

What is the price of a hug?
If it belongs to the past,
a hug is just a hug,
maybe even simulated and if it lasts.

In times of waste,
those arms interlocked
were undervalued,
in its absence no tears in the eyes.

If you feel it deep inside
now its value multiplied
produces that burning you cannot hide
filled with pure hope.

We have lived in dreams
yearning for the past,
again I have you in front of me
I might not be aware of the blast,
of your arms interlocked
picking up the pieces
from those badly given hugs and kisses
traded for scratches but not blisses.

And if I sit you down by my side
the heart speeds up

for the well-earned hugs
that will not be postponed.

XXIII. HOPE

The treasured riches are valued
when at the bottom of our worries
they are sinking in a hurry.
The wind does not bend to hope
because hope always resists the storm.

This life lesson
should never go unnoticed,
nor turn the other cheek.
Always with your circumstances
you have to be strong, not just pretend,
fight and ride the waves
against the current.

We have to get up a hundred times,
even if you stumble a thousand times in your life,
even though this opponent
fight like a corsair.

Don't push your luck
and fight with a sword… and your teeth.
Luck turns its back on the weak
and you are the buccaneer
who puts the sabre in his mouth
so as not to be left to chance.

Think of this contest
will be difficult to assault
although if you fight from the top
you will get the miles you earned
to reconcile you with your battles.

We are returning to a new life
don't leave the sail of your destiny
blow on its own free will,
skillfully take the helm
and take the course of your existence
to reach the next breakwater.

Always sail downwind
without ever turning upwind
do not allow to list
your ship skirting the harbor of misery,
let the keel sail smoothly
among your deepest problems
but don't lose your way
so you never have to say…
I'm falling apart.
Keep the word despair away from your journey
and hoist the flag of optimism
throwing you on board…
for yourself.

XXIV. TO PETS ORPHANED BY THE VIRUS

Today I die with you
sad and tired,
sad because you left me,
sad because you left,
and you only took a one-way ticket
removing happiness from my life.

Now, behind these cold bars
I miss yesterday's awakening
when you caressed my being
And I was scratching your skin with my whiskers.

Just a glimpse
was enough to understand each other,
that seemed to last… forever
and you see… eternity is non-existent
in this paper-fragile hell,
silencing our romantic ballad in an instant.

You, without words
Me, at your feet
unable to take my eyes out of you
waiting for you to open me the door.

Then on the street
overjoyed
jumping up and down
deeply grateful to you and your love.

But now, you are no longer here
and a pang of loneliness swept over me,
unjust loneliness…
Hopefully we would be able to start over,
If our paths will cross once again
in the far beyond…
Crying in the shadow of our memories of happiness.

NEW TIMES FOR ANOTHER CHANCE

The glass of wine that Barbara offered Alvaro not only contained the dark cherry-toned elixir that characterizes a good Reserva wine, it also embraced the hope of a reunion, after more than two months without seeing her ex-husband. She had invited him to dinner to sign the divorce, which was due to complete before the confinement. But the real motives were quite different…

Before taking his first sip, Alvaro swirled the wine around in the glass to smell the bouquet and rested his nose on the brim of the glass… How many memories were evoked by that unmistakable smell of ripe red fruits, sweet spices and chocolate, mixed with the perfume of Chanel number 22 that Barbara was wearing. Alvaro was the sort of person who thought: «Be careful placing your trust in someone who doesn't like wine».

The long evening ended but the night still seemed young. Alvaro excused himself for a moment to go to the bathroom, and Barbara took the opportunity to settle down on the sofa, half-naked and dressed in her fine red passionate lingerie. As she waited impatiently, she thought of how many times they had enjoyed such evenings with a good bottle of wine.

Alvaro stumbled his way into the room, the brightness of the streetlight flooded through the window, piercing the curtains, the sound off the raindrops could be heard like chimes at a relaxing concert. Barbara had left the blind and the curtain deliberately open, so that later the light would dare to uncover her body. In another time, when love reigned between the two of them, they used to hear this sound together, as they lay huddled, carried away by its deceptive harmony, although these were better times. Now austerity was mastering their relationship.

Lying on the sofa, she waited for her husband's vision to become accustomed to the gloom so he could look at her lying there in a provocative attitude, her lingerie hinting at sex, and that was what she has been waiting for, for so long. The desire to please him had become the same as the desire to feel him. When their gazes crossed, words were left over. Two bodies looking for complicity. She closed her eyes, hoping for lips that would kiss her with passion. Alvaro brushed her neck gently with his tongue and with light bites he went looking for her mouth eager and full of desire, still tasting the fruit, wood's vanilla flavour and the perfect acidity of his favourite wine.

Forgetting about time, their skins started blending and his hands slowly flew towards Barbara's swollen breasts, which was one of her most erogenous and sensitive areas. He knew well how to caress her and she let herself be carried away in a submissive way, while he was opening a way between her legs. He stopped just as he reached the navel with his fingers, sliding his body and inviting her to turn around and lie on her stomach, so that he could slowly move his lips around her back until he reached the area that provoked the most sensuality in Alvaro. His buttocks unbalanced the fieriness, so he remained for a few minutes recreating himself with adoration.

Then he turned her over on his chest and for a few seconds the world ceased to exist...just two excited bodies rubbing against each other to the rhythm of a subtle yet wild melody, until they reach the point where orgasm becomes pleasure. That pleasure that makes you climb to the clouds and by the time you come down you feel exhausted but happy, the happiness that gives you the security of having wasted passion plus the passion received. Alvaro and Barbara agreed on this way of thinking, affirming that full happiness can only be achieved with sex and a good bottle of wine.

And it all started with another chance for love and hope...

Índice

About the author

Juan Antonio Almanado enjoys expressing his feelings in words. Despite the adolescence of his writing, he already has several works in project, apart from this book of poems which is a faithful reflection of the experiences lived during the Covid-19 pandemic and his first published book. On one hand, a novel with the Second World War as a backdrop, and on the other hand, a second book of poetry, where he lets out all his words in the direction of the reader's mind.